Praise for *The Years of Blood*

"Evil is a question for God and beauty emerges despite what the politicians have ruined. . . . In this harrowing collection, Agarau shapes and sifts through shadow until light treads steadily home." —Remica Bingham-Risher, author of *Room Swept Home*

"With exquisite sensitivity, rigorous measure, and steadfastness, Agarau writes a history in which the personal and lyrical necessarily run through its marrow." —aracelis girmay, author of *the black maria*

"In a world that clamors for universality, Agarau looks within—invested in bringing to mind the beauty and brutality of his community, reminding us that humans are more alike than they are not." —D. M. Aderibigbe, author of *How the End First Showed*

The Years of Blood

POETIC JUSTICE INSTITUTE

Elisabeth Frost, *series editor*

The Years of Blood

poems

Adedayo Agarau

Fordham University Press   New York   2025

Fordham University Press has no responsibility for the persistence or accuracy of URLs for external or third-party Internet websites referred to in this publication and does not guarantee that any content on such websites is, or will remain, accurate or appropriate.

Fordham University Press also publishes its books in a variety of electronic formats. Some content that appears in print may not be available in electronic books.

Visit us online at www.fordhampress.com.

For EU safety / GPSR concerns: Fordham University Press, Joseph A. Martino Hall, 45 Columbus Avenue, 3rd Floor, New York, NY 10023, fordhampress@fordham.edu

Library of Congress Cataloging-in-Publication Data available online at https://catalog.loc.gov.

Printed in the United States of America

27 26 25   5 4 3 2 1

First edition

For Ìbàdàn—city of my youth, and for the children who built it.

Contents

iii

iv

The Years of Blood

Wind

It could be me whose blood is crying. A pestle pounding a skull in a mortar. It could be my father who is not coming home tonight. Or sister, who is raped, her breasts sliced clean, her pubic hair shaved, her body dumped in a bush near Liberty Stadium. It could be my mother's headless body we gather around in the morning. Somewhere, a mother is throwing herself to the ground in someone's house. She is screaming, *oró ò!* the dart of pain bull's-eyeing her heart. It could be my ghost finding the touch of its mother in a house where the doors are shutting against the portals of grief. I could be coming through the window as wind. I could be filling the room with cold. I could be whispering *I am here* and my mother is not hearing. Weak in her grief, she could be staring at the wall where my ghost is standing, calling my name, saying, *ọmọ mi dà? Come to mummy.* A father of four intact bodies could be giggling under his breath, whispering to his friend that *wèrè lòún yà lọ yìí,* which means *she is running mad.* There is a story of a shovel filling a body with dust.

i

Ìbàdàn

everywhere weed grows is a wild mouth eating children

there are flowers you can't touch   outside someone's house

at night, a mother

pounds the head of her newborn   at first, it is music   then the silence of crickets

we gather dust sand   murals wilt flowers   worn sandals iron cast Ìbàdàn over dreams

we collect the first fruits   ones older women snatch from us in sacred rooms

fried in sin

        my aunt's husband sacrifices her for riches   the shade of shadows stands still

in his courtyard

we no longer go to their house   no longer eat the food   my cousins bring

in baskets covered with hand towels

i kick a frog out of my slippers   put saliva on my wound   leave for school the morning i

was kidnapped

& when they found me   i was standing by a *NEPA* pole insensible   the window of

grief that opened in my family   shut itself & opened in a house down the street   children

began to die then

we could no longer go to the playfield at dusk to run & sing & dance & call someone *ojuju*

& watch them cry

      & sing them *sakasakashushu*

         everywhere weed grows is a wild mouth eating children

i dream that someone carves out my friend's eye from its cavity & the next day he is lost forever

what do i know about leaving that held the hands that snatched me?

we gather dust for bodies that never make it home

        pray over their bodiless graves, wash our hands in the river down the road

    & lock ourselves in

Sọ̀kà

"Several parents, especially women, could only
use photographs to identify their wards. Years
of separation have erased some of the signs they
could use to identify their wards."
— THE VANGUARD

A machete cutting deep through
the bones of a child
is someone else's answered prayer.

They found dried bones of people's children
a heap of old clothes, and over the rusty knives
gleaming in the small light leaning in through

the crack in the rough drywall of the *forest*,
a lizard swallows an insect and nods.

God is somewhere withering in his envelope of silence,
following a cry for help. The echoes, as reported, were
ghastly, ghostly.

In a corner, a ridge of brown shorts and baby diapers sits
beside a dying woman. There were school uniforms
and leather bags and plastic bottles and sandals and
books and mats and bras and metal bowls and buckets

and a girl, 14, thin with homesickness, breastfeeding a child.
In another room, they found femurs, the latitude of suffering
and tenderized beef served in calabashes,

dove's feathers, pigeons and their severed heads,
intestines of nameless mammals, blood in plastic bags,
heads of different sizes, and bodies lying lifelessly on altars.

We daydreamed of angels

Months later, the echoes. We were still tilling the fields in that dream,
searching for whistles in the wind. Our parents doubted the flood that had
overrun the city. Later, they screamed at us to run and fill our clothes with air.
We went to church with them and prayed. They hosted vigils on the streets
while some fathers who didn't care about god drank gin and chatted
with other fathers who didn't care about god. The tires burning all night
blued into the forenoon sky. The river flowing past our street dumped
decomposing cadavers of children kidnapped. And like phrases, their bodies,
an incomplete sentence. The hot air in the afternoon swept silence through
our empty soccer field. We watched the news at 7 for familiar names of lost friends.
Our mothers plaited our hair rough & made us cold *zobo*. We daydreamed of
angels through our father's windows and watched birds perch on clotheslines
as the sun sank into oblivion.

Unfound

there was aching in the minaret's call that evening. we saw it in feet quickened

toward prayer, the hollowed throats, the panting for water, the sun sinking in the bowels of clouds,

the gentle wind sweeping the street as if cleansing the hands that took & took, the eyes

narrowed into the doorknob twisting the body of someone's son into shadow, the flames

of memories & a silhouette of grief, the wildfire of silence touching everyone's house, the prayer

points from the church down the street, & the desperation in the hands of mothers rocking the

pictures of their sons. there were dreams in which the sons were no longer sons, in which

they were quickened steps, in which they were the cleric's tasbih counted in prayer,

in which their sisters were calling their names & there were echoes calling back at the girls—

between loss & grief, the heavier is one whose body morphed into decibels of sorrow—that evening

the party searched the street, the uncompleted building where they had found his school uniform
earlier,

searched the tiny paths that led to the river that flowed from the end of the city, checked

the police station, searched his mother's room, under her bed, inside her purse, followed the steps

quickened toward prayer, into the hollowed throat of the mother panting for her son.

In which the morning after, a boy's body had been dismembered

To God who made me, the clouds move toward us on that field.
It has just rained & the street is flooded again.
A boy whose face I do not remember has been dancing in
the rain & has now caught a cold.
We gather around him as good friends do & because he sneezes, we sneeze.
As our shadows fall into the corridors of our fathers' house,
we ask ourselves what we want to become in the future.
One says *police*. Another says *pilot*. I say I want to be a thief. We laugh.
I want to run all my life because I have seen the magic wind does to a garment in motion.
We gather our feet and count. & because "even number" rhymes with "evil number,"
you are a thief, the game master calls. Because "odd" rhymes with "Lord,"
you are catching the thieves. We sort into our numbers.
At the count of three, we go into hiding, he commands. We begin the search of our lives,
running from corridor to corridor, searching. Little boys of this world tending
to desire the way god tended the garden. Because I want to be found, I sneeze.
The boy carrying the wood shaped like a gun has so much compassion
& he can't shoot at me. He smiles and keeps running. Later, it becomes fully dark
& the moon stands by watching our performance of escape. Our mothers,
who have finished cooking dinner, bring their benches & sit outside, watching
the galore of night dancers. The wind arrives briefly, and we trace the dark with our hands.
    When we
finally tire & our breathing arrives together, we gather in a circle, our feet touching.
& as we begin to count, a boy says, *the last to get home is a fool.*

Empty

We begin gently,
        go into the day like a prayer.
Hands stretching to collect
        also stretch to take. Our friend
leaves school & does not reach home.
        We search the street, & field, empty.
We do not find his body.
        Months later, they dug him a grave
at the Òkè Bọ́là Cemetery.
        His brother, Jay Jay, wears a suit
& his mother's face shrinks in gloom.
        My friends & I stare into the silence
filling his coffin, the farewells that follow.
        The fire in his daddy's eyes
meets the pastor's prayers
dropping into empty open palms.
The moon leans upon the small stream
        the night we cover his grave.

Ghost of a Dead Boy Writes from Sòkà

In the gloaming, algae on the walls blossom. A bowl of
blood is a festering—a child's skull is a new path.
Yellow chrysanthemums wilt as wind flares
the embers of this cataclysm—I can see
my mother's hands, the way they break groundnuts open.
I met a girl here whose smile, in the scorn of this house,
reminds me of you. The bones on the ground,
dried femurs of diminutive dreams, rinse their teeth
with blood. How are you? We arrive numb, forgetful
of home, & are sat in the dark. Cockerels & crickets,
turning time within us. Sometimes, the sound of drums
from the church beside the forest drowns this muffling shrine.
When it's loudest is when the saw begins to sink. My
mother, how is she? Tell her I came home a few times,
touched her skin & left. I dream of flowers & empty
houses & barns of yam & breaktime at BODMA.
I dream of you. Light seeps out of my body as my blood calls your name.
Once, a band of boys was delivered in the evening. One of them
was someone I know from Ogunleye Street. Fola, his dreads
short & his uniform untidy. Because I can no longer speak, I

nod at him. His eyes, full of fear, acknowledge the terror.
Where did they catch you, I mouth. I pretend we are on that lawn
near the police station, playing football, cloaked in sweat. I'm happy to see you.

hoax

yesterday, a small-bodied thing of joy
today, a bucket of blood & bones
and a new moon glowing outside.

they are pounding the bone
with a pestle—

bringing feathers
to the fire
       where a body is burning—

       desire brought before light
in incantations
       the hawk's dream is to rattle the snake with abjection
the snake's prayer is to crawl over the rock unnoticed—

who in the room is singing nightingale
       strumming silence
           in a language wet with loss

turning

our eyes into a flood—

    the mortar sings to the bones, *gbomgbom gbomgbom*

& the bones listen   to the fervency of anguish

by the time the ritual ends

the baby's mother will   cry

out of sleep—the road   will

burn—who bites the bones

when the body

    crumbles?

Salt water

For Michael Shotinbo

The door opens and you are there, plucking cobwebs. My father says when a spider builds a home, it's to catch a fly. I agree. Somehow, in the dark, your voice follows me. An angel missing is a point mistaken for an answer. A shadow misconstrued as a hue. We didn't stop searching. Even after they found your bleached body in the river we used to swim, your mother, in disbelief, hushed us back to the street. Michael, we don't go to the field anymore. They say the hands that snatched you will snatch children till democracy arrives. Till the soldiers on Òkè-Àdó return to their barracks & the news informs us we have a president. In fact, after democracy arrives, politicians will need to stay in power. Instead of music, my father's old radio reports missing people. They say a pregnant woman was hacked on College Crescent. They carved open her cavity & took the fetus. Can you hear me knocking on God's door, asking if you are okay? Did you make it home whole, like the silence after a long sentence? My grandfather asked my mother to bathe us in salt water for protection. If you can read this, my grandfather told my mother to tell us to bathe in salt water. That no evil shall befall us again.

Bámiṣé

*"Bámiṣé (Olúwabámiṣé) Tóyọ̀sí Àyánwọlé was a
young Nigerian woman who was abducted after
boarding a BRT in Lagos, Nigeria, and found
dead 9 days later."*

—LINDA IKEJI

the hands salting the sea bring brass into the night—

    the fervor of light we must carry to be found wanting,

the pound of flesh, the latitude of need

whose hands are these that house these yearnings

    who spits against the wall, what song must the body mime

to survive the threnodies of ritual?

tonight an uncouth dog is barking in the dark;

    half of her tongue dips in fear   her body palpitating

in a bus where there is shadow, a plenitude of empty seats

one woman & two other men. what we do not know

    is what labyrinths we must map to walk through bones;

to wake in a city grappling with the skulls of children snatched from their mother's backs. at the climax of dusk,

      her body is learning to singe with blade; it is slowly charring

as she is made to sit over a pot of her blood.

a breath exits the gates of her body

      before the body tears through the wooden doors

where retributions are seized with a grapnel.

in the soft light of dawn, there is a man pouring

      incantations over her lifeless body;

another slicing her breasts into a bowl.

what prayers she must have screamed,

      what inches of nails in the palm of her god;

we heard the scream, but the aftermath of her silence . . .

Night, prayer

I wait for God's
response. In the hush
of the dark, the candle's
fire dances.
Be careful. That it glows
does not mean
it isn't in flames.
The gecko on the wall nods
as it swallows a fly.
Is this a sign
that predators also pray
for blossom?
In the next room, my father
snorts in his sleep.
I hear the turning,
hear the whistle outside.
They are burning
tires so the smell of butadiene
rubber and carbon
black fills our room.
It's been two weeks, and Michael
has not been found.
Small fires are everywhere—

under the bushel,
in someone's house,
in my parents' marriage.
I ask God to find the edge
and trim our fire.
As an answered prayer
wind arrives,
blows the candle out.

Portent

They smeared a widowed cockerel's blood at the end of the street.
They buried a goat's placenta by the small gate erected by the small pool
linking our street with the NTC road and Liberty Stadium. Decked
in white & the glory of cowries, eyes bloodshot as their tongues rolled
in incantations, the priests walked with measured gait down the street. A small
boy carried a calabash containing three wraps of molded cornmeal, a smear of palm oil
& seven bean cakes. The priests swore blood was an antidote to disappearance.
Spat gin on walls & told us to go to bed. What we learned regarding rituals is that blood
is thicker than blood. That night, gunshots spoiled the night with fear. Birds the next
morning cried like wolves, like the woman whose children were shot in their sleep.

ii

Boys who never die

after Safia Elhillo

Boys who dance
around plastic chairs
in front of the barbers' shops
to win a free haircut.

Boys who gaze at the moon
& fabricate a story
about the man who left his mother &
turned into a Moonman.

Boys who love their mothers and
run after cows on Ogunleye Street.

When ice cream melts and slings down the arm,
the boys lick their arms. Corn boys. Yam boys.
Boys who never joke with food.

Boys who show us new shoes their father got them.
Joyous boys, laughing like the sea.
Boys who call me *friend*.
Boys who buy me sweet, goodie-goodie.

25

Quadri, Olúṣhọlá, Adams, Ògúnkọ̀yà, Saheed Apárí, Pẹ́ńkà,
Adémọ́lá, Oluwatosin, Mido, Ṣẹ́gun, Ọládèjì,
Káyọ̀dé Kareem, Adéwùsì Ṣèyí, Bùkọ́lá, Victor Ọlátúnjí, Olúṣhọlá
Dámilọ́lá, James, Tọ́lá, Dáramọ́lá, Taofeek, Ibrahim

Boys puzzled by god's grace.
Boys who open their eyes during prayers.

Boys in love with the same girls.
Boys fighting over girls.
Boys without flowers, boys with flowers.
Boys who love boys
Boys who love boys who love boys
Boys who hide. Boys who seek.
Boys jumping thin lines of life playing *sùwé*.
Snake and Ladder boys.
Boys watching their father's fathers play draught.
Pàrágà boys. Boys who like the smell of cigarette
but swear they'll never smoke.
Boys who fill ground chalk in rolled paper &
puff. Boys in a kitchen filled with smoke.
Boys who carry scars from playgrounds.
Boys who carry scars their fathers give them.

Boys who don't listen. Boys who listen.
Boys who revolt. Boys who leave home.

Boys who will never be absent like their fathers
Boys who watch their fathers at bars down the street
Boys who search for their fathers in the dark.
Hungry boys. Dreamy boys. Boys who teach boys how to wank.

Boys kissed by older women. Boys kissed by young women.
Boys the hope of a chameleon—
always changing, always changing.
Saturday boys dancing to Ebenezer Obey. *Tom and Jerry* boys
Saturday Special on BCOS. *World Wide Wrestling* with Shaun Michaels.
Tinko-tinko boys. Boys who love bright colors.
I wear yellow & you wear sky blue.
Little stars dotting the sky. Noisy boys.
Boys who kiss boys who kiss girls.
Boys who love God and go to church in their best shoes.
Homeboys. Street boys.
Boys who leave home for school one morning,
Their corrupted bodies litter a small farm days after.

Entrance

; / because the body does not listen / it ends. because the body listens / it ends. again / my family is in my dream picking apples in a cider orchard / my sister runs out of the dream / my brother chases her

; / we bring nothing before everything / piece the wooden horse & set the road on fire / sing as clouds grumble / scrub our eyes clean of dreams / my father places his right hand on my shoulder & / my mother waves at us

; / the truth is that i do not identify a journey until i'm stuck / i'm singing wisps & strumming bees / i lead a flock of children out of the priory & give them names / my brother calls my name as i turn the boat into a bed / in the deep of sleep the water wavers over the body / my father snores in a storm / my mother slashes the paperwall with a sledgehammer / am i dreaming of ways to bury the flocks / dreaming of ways to bury my friends / my sister sings from inside the church & its pews hum along / there is no saving for a fish spat out of water / in the drowning i ask air what it takes to be everywhere / enquire of the heaviness of wreckage / my mother waves again / my brother comes out of our old house with a chicken / thunder slices its throat & we are in a feast / there is laughter bliss & music syncing with the burns in my chest / i vomit

wool / vomit my grandmother's pendant / vomit the promise
/ to keep my friend alive / he calls my name & i answer / he
calls again as the door leading out of the city opens / he calls
again

; / in the dark / bruised bones apologize to flesh / i turn the
boat toward an uncertain place / the silt river wets my face &
my mouth bitters / a star trips & shuts the door / my window
of escape is a nestling / i call a dove out of my hands / twist
the neck / perform my ablution / the ground hawks the dove's
blood back into my hands / i know the graves i have made
myself are why my body is never at rest / tínko tìnko tìnkoko
tìnko—the flock of children sizzles a kind of prayer / i pace
toward the small trance of light / a voice the size of god
turns me back / i sit waiting for a shadow to form / i form a
performance of waiting

Sonnet with Blood Everywhere

still, blood pruned from old stalks—still, the ghost
        singing outside the boulevard
—still the bombed cathedral hammocked to my body—
        still the howling choir of adolescent boys
—their assaulted throats their troubling tongues—still
        the eyes peeping through the keyhole—the
naked woman inside the bathroom stilling the naked boy inside—
        still a still monochrome photo of joy
burning in the cathedral half rented by memory—still ceramic walls in the bath
        room—still the menstrual blood in the tub i'm still deep inside—still i sink
still i sing till i surface—still i stink—still the
        breathless boy still longing, still waking on the street
of still desires borrowed—still the pleas in the nightmare—
        still *please take the apology & burn memory*

Fine boy writes a poem about anxiety

i.

i ask my girlfriend to pray for me & she pulls my name in a two-minute voice note
throws me toward heaven & receives me with gratitude

i miss everything i worship:
      a. my God
      b. my woman
      c. my mother & grandmother
      d. the music flaming from rooms we bless with the heat of our bodies

the way i desire her body is the way anxiety desires me
      i am wanted by all the things that haunt me in my dream

my grandmother, my grandmother
pulling me out of air

ii.

> on a sidewalk on 7th street
> a dead cat is someone's pet

in Ìbàdàn, a dead cat
is someone's grandmother

iii.

      as a fine boy, kò yẹ kí o ní anxiety nau
      o ní everything tí o fẹ́, ó yẹ kí o máa dúpẹ́ ni

i thank my God who puts sunlight on my table
who wakes me in the morning & offers me to trembling

who sits outside the apartment near River Landing
smoking a stick of cigarette with menthol switch

who asks me how Nigeria is
who, when i say *dáadáa ni,*

does not ask what i mean

iv.

there is little i can tell you, the anger is toward the door that never opens inside me; i make eba in the morning & vomit everything later & when my mother calls, she asks why i'm thinner than hair

v.

1. where will all fear go when god takes over the city?
2. whose gratitude will drive the lambs into the swine?
3. what am i without the dream where i am gasping for air?
4. what name do we give the fire that eats my fingers?
5. my mother beads a basket & fills it with water,
6. who does she mock if not her son that cannot hold water?

v.

they laugh at me
when i run in
the blues of
morning.

they laugh at me
when i run in
the grey of
dark.

i hear their shadows
& dream of their socks

v.

a lizard crawls toward a car
& the driver halts.

i've witnessed a car run into a pack
of boys walking tiredly from
school.

v.

your god is everything
that lets you come inside.
mother, lover.

this trembling is
not without a destination.

Doomsday

my anxiety is that the boy walking in the snow on 7th street looks like my brother
the stars are black in the morning sky, or are the birds stuck—lost in the horizon
    where a brush is damping the clouds with grief? / mornings after an overdose
    are often blessed with the assurance that the body can take anything as long as it's
not ready to leave—the man pronounced mad by my friends appears in this
landscape with a rainbow in his mouth—*why him naked, why me sef con naked?*
    what is this orchestra of trifling illnesses growing on my head? why is
    this room turning into a field of wilting lavender—*olúwa, níbo lójú rẹ̀ wà?*
my anxiety is that the boy walking in the snow on 7th street looks like me now
i am standing by the window, watching the sky fill the earth with a precipitate
    of sorrow / a man is mowing his way through the open field / another is
    burning a lover's note. *i wan comot / i wan make flower fill me to the brim*
the way the sky fills the ground with rain / everyone is out≠in≠side
but these two men in my head—the wind folding into itself, sweeping flakes
    off the terrains that lead to the pool house / whose tongue is it that licks clean
    the blood in my hand—in which i fashion a fresh brand of desire
what i really want is that i do not wake feeling like the birds
stuck in the sky like a painting like a brush damping hues into the clouds
    but what happens is that i wake feeling like the birds stuck in a sky
    in which a brush is damping me hues into clouds / i call my mother instead the
machine answers / in stead of prayer, the desire to cut clean the disdain in my throat
where everyone con dey when baba god dey sama person door? where is salvation

on the day of reckoning—i go back to sleep

i wake in a dream where there is a knife in my palms—in which there is blood everywhere

in which a boy walking in the snow on 7th street looks like my brother

in which the stars are grey and birds are dead in my hands? their hollow bones

lost in the horizon where a brush is damping the clouds with grief? mornings after an overdos

are often blessed with the assurance that the body can take anything as long as it's

not ready to leave—i am on a field of millet in iowa with a rainbow in my mouth

i am naked, my hand reaching the echoes in the spaces light does not reach

my head a headdress with women singing a dirge—my mother, my mother, waving

her fingers in the direction the choir goes—suddenly the field of millet is

the room where i was born is the field of wilted lavender—where i am is where i am

before the audience of god, a shadow of something condemned to silence

my anxiety is that the boy walking in the snow on 7th street is me

i am standing by the window, watching the sky fill the earth with a deposition

of despair / my father is mowing his way through the open field / in my head

& i am burning an ex's note / i crawl toward the part of the field where

rain is pouring over the barn—i want to be filled with love

with the memories of blue morning & grand sex / everyone inside my head harmonizes

a song about two men in the snow—the wind folding into itself, sweeping flakes

off the terrains leading to the slaughterhouse / whose tongue is it that licks clean

the sore in my mouth—i wake up inside the bird stuck in the sky

in which the creator is painting the grief out of me as he brushes a blur

over the damnation in my wing, coloring the clouds offset white

i call my mother & she is crying, asking *how you com dey?*

Arrival

in the evening,
       clouds shiver by the door   rain pours outside the town
            òrìṣà ilé ẹni kì í hunni   but my great-aunt turns rat
poison in amala for me   my bones shake the fortitude of loss
              my mother runs outside screaming at the blood in my mouth
the river turns toward me   into a sand house
    between the sky & the cities floating beneath me, a father & a son carry shards of glass
in their bosom
     òde là ńṣàgbà, ilé kan bí ìbó; bó pe títí,
àtilé àtòde ní ḿbo wáá kàn

       my first sin was i came as a son
              arole
     the second is
         my grandfather blessed me with his final breath
ogún-mobí, ọmọ kòrikò;
ọgbon-mowò ọmọ èrúwà;
kàkà ká bí ẹgbàá bùn, ká bí
kanṣoṣo bùn, ó kúkú yá

                    a goat bleats
          aching the body
                          with redemption

Síkírá,—omo iya ʻalakara
          —my grandmother
tears her palm with a knife
          & pours herself inside my mouth

                    i came four days late
                          earth mothers spent the night
                    sealing me dead inside my mother's womb

the muezzin
mounts the
pulpit

the muezzin falls
off

          a congregation tumbles in wonder—
                    at the beginning of my life
                    my bruised life
                          the bruised almond tree dried

in the mosque where my grandfather prayed his final fajr
where, outside, beside a woman who roasted corn
& sold groundnuts, he made ablutions; the children hymned
alfathia

    al hamdu lillaahi rabbil 'alameen
ar-rahman ar-raheem maaliki yaumid deen

in the silence of solitude, the bizarre calmness of dusk, fireflies eulogize the algorithms of home
    in the dream, the hunter's gun turns toward the house of sand where my body hides its flight
        turns toward the paper boat, the abundance of brown leaves
        pans toward the choir of boys singing their lungs out of a cathedral

the day of reckoning is the day the bats find joy in their cave
    in the songs where i am searching the city for candles
        i find the wall, my grandmother's face, the lines on her cheeks,
        the map of time

i wake in the turquoise blue room
    the cat meowing as my great-aunty
& her company of witches gather around the baby cot
    picking my body out with a needle   orogún kì í jogún orogún
                                  òkò lọ mọ: ọlorun ní ńwí
                                  pé ká sọ síbi tó dára

the sea collects me from the sand house

                  my mother puts me to sleep

                                   the dream

returns

Sonnet with severed limbs

yet, the willow tears through the window whose light tilts into the room

       yet, the wind weaves ghostly the leaves—the widow's body glowing

in the incandescent light—yet, as the wound festers, the cat pulls out

       another cat's bone from under the bed—how many children came here

& never found the door—the window as high as sky—the widow as high

       as Spirit—the willow forever weaving through the spirit of loss—through

the dust in harmattan—i carry my dream with me in the dream—bring fire

       out from the pouch —[how many bones have dried in silence?]—bless the river with spit

turn toward the road that is full of boys—naked & singing—knackered & stung

       —bring from wounded years the smell of sore—cavity the memory—place it

inside a glass of water—watch it bloom in dim light—rippling as the boys

       drown—rippling as i gag—i say my name before i remember God—i say

my name before i beg the knife turned into my limbs—yet the iroko tears—

       & the wind weaves the leaves in symphonies—& the boys' bones sing, *severed, severed* . . .

Springfield

In the parking lot of 99 cents on Springfield avenue,
my father says, *nobody charges you for parking at home*

we stand outside the mall, beside his black unnumbered wagon,
talking about home & the cold hands it plunges deep
toward the ossicles of dream

in Ìbàdàn, there are no buses waiting for you,
no waiting, no lamppost on College Crescent
at 5am when your throat is thick with fog

you are not wearing three trousers
and a winter coat, you are not heavy
with desire, & you are not trapped here

wrapped inside the fond hope you carried years
before you walked before the consulate,
before sliding the white paper

beneath the glass barricade.

I wanted to be here, in this country,

to claim triumph over grief

& not worry that there is a shrine in my father's house

where an old woman is calling my name

into a calabash

the abduction

i think what i saw threw me outside the
house—i think a hand dipped into the
room through the aluminum roof—i think
the boys were playing hide & seek then—i
think their mothers were in the kitchen &
their fathers drinking at beer parlors where
younger women are rubbing their chests,
telling them stories of other men dipping
their fingers into their bowels & calling
forth water—i think the children were
singing when the hand fisted their throats—i
think their muffles were in sync with the
thuds of pestles against mortars in the
kitchen—i think the house suddenly became
desolate—& as each boy was fetched from
the house, their shadows refused to leave
the wall—i think i heard shadows wailing,
pulling the bodies from flight but unable to
hold—i think what i saw threw me out of my
dream—on a certain morning, i saw a man
sitting by the drainage on Liberty road—
his eyes swollen with questions—i think
i hastened my steps, i think i ran, i think i
didn't look back—memory forsakes the body
at the point where fear fills the body like air

It begins with gratitude & ends in rage

The arrow finds the sparrow in its wishbone—
       I am grateful it's the bird falling out of the sky
A child crawling toward fire, startled by the wonder
       of its own shadow, waits & waits
I am grateful I didn't find the long throat of sea or
       that it didn't swallow me because
everything the water touches, it keeps—
       my uncle who left home one morning
was found washed clean in a gully after the flood.
       I am grateful for the spring & the pendulum,
the cannibal's teeth broken by my infant bone.
       In the small room, my father starts a prayer
& stops somewhere between the promises of God
       lost like his brother & the pleas for revival
my mother heaves a sigh, takes the baton of prayer
       into her muzzle, & closes it.
I am grateful that I have been given this day, dear Lord,
       grateful the fire touched me & blessed me with
scars—& dreams where i am planting myself
       in a stranger's field of daffodils, or a mile away

from the battlefield—I know nothing of the battles
      i am fighting, what do I know of the blood
that flows through me? What do I know of this name,
Adédayọ̀, that as I walk toward the playfield,
arrows follow me? The salt of àge sprinkled over
      the undying wounds years gave me. My
Lord, my shepherd is sleeping
      without his flock of children as
the bird drops into sea.

Baba omo

a rampaging wind sweeps the street clean, sweeps the ghosts
out of their white shawls, sweeps light into the corners where
the cigar burns—where a flurry of flame is exhaled—hope
hanging loosely between two fingers, raising a stick toward
a mouth, the wind mops dust off the bodies attempting to
rise, pulling a sleeve song upon themselves—the wind
felons, pinching the gentle night into a stranger
thing—a child babbles from inside a house & the mother lifts
it from its cot & rocks it in her hand—the wind sweeps itself
toward their door, knocks like a father
searching the wall for an entrance into his old parlor, the
wind raging, turning outside beside the halogen lamppost
whose light spoils the decorum of darkness—the road is tarred
but no one is plying it, only the emerging bones, only the father
who hears—from a strange city—his child crying in the dross of night.

Two Boys, Their Mother & the Face

two boys are throwing
stones into the river—
their mother is beating
colored dresses against
a small rock—there is a
dye in the stream—an
unfamiliar face splashes
against the surface of the
stream—the afternoon heat
steams toward god—then
darkness happens—then
we are taken into the
room where the woman is
sitting in a corner—calling
her children, waiting
for their voices, or their
footsteps—through the
small window we see a
man fixing his roof—the
trees that line Fẹ̀lẹ̀lẹ̀
are palms and baobabs
leaning into silence—the
wind weaving a song with
their branches—when the
echoes arrive the woman is
sleeping—it's her innocence
to absence, the opaqueness

of rain filling her dream—
when the echoes arrive the
woman is sleeping dreaming
of her boys throwing stones
in the river where she beats
colored cloths against the
rock—where an unfamiliar
face fills the shallow with
thirst—

Disappearance

After God's approval of that trial, I stopped trusting the hands that promised to hold me.
The body a bridge   at the end of it, a camp on fire.   I stare at the staggering smoke,

wondering whose child is ashing, waiting for the father who limps out, shouting, *omo mi, omo mi*.
Pastors promised that God does not leave *their* children. In the dream that I fall off

the tree, my head squashes on the pavement before my grandmother's house. The puree
of blood, the years squeezed into rage.   My mother's groanings with my father's mourning are

distilled into a single sigh. I'd like to know what the fire seeks when the body is burning. I want to ask
what God inquires when *their* children are tried. The loyalty of fire to scour clean disbelief or [
].

iii

Before the dark

the antelope's ribcage, a bridge of bones at the base of the anthill—
        you are outside your father's house that is outside the city that is
outside the country where a bullet dislodges an infant's bone—the
        owls are learning about the dunes of night, the terrain is full of
widowed birds searching the bark of trees for holes—boys your age
        are somewhere afar, before a river waiting to lick them off
of their salt—the throes mothers carry in the place you are from
        are remembered by the number of boys who fell off their backs before
they named them—before the dark, the sun is setting the sky on
        fire—pink flames burning the clouds, a bird is crashing, the storm
coming carries the face of the people in your dreams where the
        antelope leaps with a bullet in its brain—where your mother
is singing a song —*the storm is coming,* the storm is coming & it is
        bringing the dark with it—dust comes before the road is forgotten
before the green of august ashes into brown november—the smell
        of rain whets your nose—as you walk inside the house, hope swallows you.

Ruin

all the light in the room being gulped by the spider—
   —the grace & prayers, ògo àti àdàbà
when the lizard diminished into the wall, when
    the music softened into echoes
when the woman slowly left her body, the glory of
    light filled the house & the spider knotted
its web across the corridors of the room,
    light filled the house & ate everything
that stayed—poems drowning in a narrow tube of books
—books consumed by dust—dust filtered into
the room through the unclosed window

Wishbone

They sit, all of them, before the photographer—who is adjusting the aperture, the neck of focus
Yet, the entrance of light steered onto the stage gathers in it a crater of dust

a woman/the mother, in a yellow dry lace & orange damask *gele*, is at the epicenter
her husband, someone's father, drizzles a smile upon the field of his face; he holds the

woman/his wife & they hold their children—one of them is a boy in whose eyes
a rainbow is knifed into a slice of lemon, in whose body is a masquerade dancing dust into

years of memory. The camera shutters the man out, his dress, purple in the first take, ashes.
The woman occupies the space that he leaves, & the children sit beside their mother/the
    woman.

Now, the boy starts a song, fills his mouth with a stash of feathers, briefly lending his throat
the audacity of gratitude; the ash remains of what the fire left when it caught the man/the
    father

out of the photo. The light takes itself out & in the loom of darkness, someone's child is
calling for help, & someone's mother is clutching space in search of her children. A requiem
    begins

from the leg of a girl/the mother's daughter/the boy's sister who morphs into a stone &

from her wrist, a bouquet emerges, & in that darkness that has fallen upon the stage, we can
    hear the grief

loud as the thud of a bird, its wishbone broken into tiny stars splattered across a hazy sky

on the night the field of millet catches fire, on the night *esu laalu ogirioko* harvests with
    flames in his mouth.

I have watched this play over & over, pulled the wishbone out of the bones of wish & said

I want my father to be here to see that darkness is fetched by the disappearance of light. I have
    tendered

mercies toward the door & forgiven the knob's twist, I have forgiven the photos & the

memories of still, the evening baked in silence & the gatherers of grief. I have forgiven deities

& mothers whose hands are soaked in my sister's blood, whose teeth are stuck in her neck,

I have forgiven the shadow of darkness & the hills of bones. The bird is always falling.

Out of the sky. I wake from the dream where my father kneels before the gods of doors.

Before the windowsill & the effigies of parting, the dried bones of my sister's absence ache.

The Dark

A bridegroom stands at the altar of waiting, his eyes
a longing the depth of woods, his hands a shiver

emerging from water. At first, I was not in that dream but you
were, walking the animal of desire through the aisle, seated on

the pews were people whose faces were birthmarks etched with
grief. I think I saw a man nodding to the brief catalog of wounds

your legs archived; an animal limping inside you, gunned by regrets
owed to a battered childhood where war claimed everything that had a name.

The limping is with blood, the blood is my father, & in my father
is a child I cannot give name to, I am pulled from a farm of maize

into a pocket of shrill. I want to be remembered by the hands, tattooed
in henna, dipped into the pocket searching for my arm. I want to be

gathered out of the storm fastening my memories to dreams where i am
alone in the museum of bones, the relics of home on the night the soldiers

stirred the river, the night the moon hid behind clouds, the night the stars
fell, one after the other, into the pool of fire; the ashing of bodies claimed

in their own houses. I want to be remembered in my own dream, by the grief
that filled my hands, once a bouquet of flowers turned toward the altar in the dream

where a little boy staggers out of the stage into a backdrop of silence.
The dark eating him, & outside, his father shouts, *tell me how to save you.*

The fig

instead the fig's fruits are stolen / a body is forsaken of its own magic

        / you bless the boy before you ask why he is lost / your

thirst is prayed over / draw water from your father's well / the grave is shut

before the bones arrive / the names are lost on the sea's tongue

the road is fogged & the body refuses the journey / heaven

        sighs over the city of your throat / the bell dings & the church

opens / you pray the woman into barrenness instead / make symphonies

from the desires of the disciples / turn the market into a congregation

/ leave the sandals outside the city & walk toward hunger / love yourself be selfless

    love the fig unable to feed the mileage of your body / ask god to command

the wood to protest as nails inch into your palms into the wood / in this poem you do

not die / you are in the synagogue not the sepulcher of dusk / telling children the parable

in which the fig's fruits were snatched & you [pray] comfort [into] the mother / in which

        someone's mother is not condemned for sleeping as her baby wanders / in which

the son is gone / & a mother dissolves into the heaviness of her heart

In which the horse saddles

ẹyín ènìyàn olúwa, as the eye of the needle finds the tongue of the thread
whose child is sinking in owl's eyes, whose child is drowning in a book

the history of knives sinks deep into the skin, the throat's refusal to pour
the poetry of blood over the tall field of grass—somewhere a mother's joy,

somewhere a mother's joy is unknitted with care—as the body finds rest
inside the cathedral of moon, whose light dies in solitude, whose light

dies with a mass of singers—the song we find here is the song that buries
a bird—ìgbà òjò ńlọ, ìgbà erùn ńlọ, a ní ká dí isà eku kó le; ìgbà wo la

óò tó wá peku náà—outside the stead, the gathering of horses, out
side the stead the gatherers of horses—i bring myself toward the knife

& turn the heat toward my mother—whose prayer will set the sky
on fire?—whose worship will sink the ghost before it finds the child?

i ask you what it means to triumph over the fire scouring the tall fields
who was it this language blessed with reverence—whose child will mother

the dead boy singing outside the confine of my dream—i throw the drawer

into the well—answer me, ẹyín ènìyàn olúwa, what will the pulley pull

out of me?

In the dark

if, for example, hope is a tangible thing, it is then the house you are walking into

—your father's house, the corridor a moving cloud at night, the walls a conglomerate

of eyes. but hope is not tangible. you are holding your body as the space widens & contracts.

the voices echoing your name. you hear them. outside the wind is gathering its children, wading

them toward the door. the storm is calling the lightning over the phone. the thunder speaks

from the other side of oblivion, cracks open the open sky. the lamps glowing softly before you

suddenly die. the gods hanging at the door scatter their feet as they run, the wind withering their
wings

swells their cloaks. you are in the dark now & the voices begin to form a face. you recognize the
first embalmed

body stumping out of the wall. the next you do not know. the rest are faces familiar from dreams
where you

are a group of boys drowning in a lake—where the cathedral is crumbling & you are inside it—
where you lead

a choir of silence & at a carol, your hands are wet with a cat's blood. you are asking what you've
done to

own this darkness, *why is my mouth full of knives?* You plead. there was a battle at the beginning
where

you cast a net into a sea of earth mothers—*who showed you the road toward this house? who pointed
you to the door? on whose grave did you slough the cat's neck? where is my blood in yours?* your great-

aunty asks. thunder speaks from the other side of the desolate town & breaks open the

walls & sends lightning into the corridor, a moving cloud at night.

Pariboto riboto

the cargo arrives just as the slices of yam are brought to boil
a father's song echoes a ferocious aching
the drums are full of rain & the child
arrives tender

the hawk must not enter
the house & the boy must
not leave his mother
until the water breaks
until the coin folds into
an eye

the cargo arrives
in a wrecked ship

the child
at bay

the mother
at sea

Lilac

the upturned field of green listens
      & the slant hibiscus swells with silence—a song stings backward

your grandfather blows dust off his own bones
      alive, the bones ache—his eyes' sockets wilt the leaves & the eyeballs push out

the sky, swirling blue winds, dunes clouds eastward
      in the distance, you see yourself walking toward the upturned field of green

listening as the slant hibiscus swells with silence
      your grandfather unmakes the words, unwrites the lyrics & the debris of memory

becomes the fog before you, a ship crushing in the wind;
      from the lavender farm, the bones are shaking & forming
            —a mother calling with echoes in her throat

//

you squint into the fog, hearing the rancorous talking drum
      saying a proverb in reverse—a door is waiting with a church of boys

///

on the lavender farm where you are also tilling the soil
        someone is unmaking love with you, taking their kiss from your mouth, unsticking

their tongue from your tongue, planting the lilac elsewhere
        their feet removing prints from the door & the language of loss

in the horrendous wind finds the farm
        finds the mother with a baby strapped to her back & fills her echoes with echoes

sweeps clean everything you see in the distance;
        —lilac
            —lavender
                —birds on the twigs of dry trees
                    —the talking drum's reversed proverbs

////

now, before you, a blue glass glows
                    with the spider's web in the sky & with promises
that were once dreams that was once a deed
            that was once a prayer

/////

in the blue glass, the sun spits out a child
        across the solemn face of the child, something, still like a lake

in the lake, your grandfather is drowning

      the bubble in your throat an empty street in winter

the lilac is without flowers—the flowers are without scent—

      a thread of rain trickles from sky, dunning clouds eastward

onto the field where you are standing

      where the bones have undone the dead & the coffin has forgiven itself

the songs have stopped—the drum a swelling foot bathed in salt

      —you are waiting with the vacancy of faith

On joy

when the news reached me, i was writing a poem on joy.
i take god out of the poem & stand it beside the
shadow of a tree i imagine as fig. i ask myself
what becomes of fire when the flame is put
to shame. i tell the shadow that light is coming.
so whose child will mourn the shadow so whose
father will bury the thirst so whose mother will
the fang of hunger find in her intestine? i want to
lift the hope from this poem & give it to the dead
person's mother, give wings to the ghost, color the
grief violet, *unsalt* the tears & teach eyes the path
out of sea, bring to the father the blueness of comfort,
teach death about itself, wreck the ship in everyone's grief.

Brown

"Eni tí ó ṣe wúrà ni wúrà ńyọ̀ lẹ́yìn rẹ̀"
—YORUBA PROVERB

somewhere before the body forms—before the mapping of desire where light uncovers the soul
the empty field sings, whittling winds with chaff wet with contempt—a god is dabbed brown

with desire—you are there in the fire, packing the ash remains of yourself. In the dream, you
are fanning the field on fire with fury—how is the god also the dog?—how is the father also the
  field

of brown, the desire also what is owned—you are outside your father's house at 3 am
  hallucinating
the shadow of a skull wearing a helmet, riding a broom, saying your name—you are walking

toward the wall that is open, from which light emerges—in the light is the girl that unbuckles
a kiss from your neck & takes desire with her—you are running after her, launching your hands

into the emptiness that they find—there is a house, a brown house, full of little boys, on fire—
where are your mothers?—you ask—you turn to a woman in a headscarf with *Bọ́là Ìgè* imprint

& you run into the house to salvage the fire instead of the boys—the boys, your face
their face—are calling your name like a rushing sea beating a rock—you run out of the house—

where the fire licks you was where the girl unbuckled her kiss—where the dream takes you is
   the graveyard

—your grandmother sitting, waiting in the dark, light in her mouth rescues the road from
   the wrath

of your feet—*sing me a song*, she says—you begin to fill your mouth with flowers but

the song is not reaching—you are singing her a song whose maladies flap in sunset—

orange yellow after the sun is in the pocket of sky—after, your shadow leaves you—after you

find yourself drowning in a pool of brown—the sky is now a rope & you are reaching & you
   are reaching—

& nothing is reaching back.

Migration

*"In a migration, only the things that are prepared
to move should be in motion."*
—SAMANTHA SCHWEBLIN

i.

the mother's body quivers in the kitchen—the tea burns her tongue
the tea kettle whistles, boiling the skin of her child—the purple kitchen
tumbles her eyes—pacing the slab, yellowish-orange sits atop the island,
waiting for hands, its shadow leaning against the wall near the window
—to be honest, what would only be lost is half of what you know—the priest
is filling the aluminum basin with distilled water once brought to boil on a
charcoal—the child is on the bed that is on a rock, breathing in the sequence
of tethered winds on a hot june afternoon—we ask who holds the earth what
hope is there for this poisoned child—what secret the dark room holds—who
is moving toward shore & who the river brings back bloated

ii.

when the chanting reaches its destination, it is without lyrics
but it is still music—so the child is still a child even if it's breathless—
even if the horses outside are dropping dead like stones landing in water—the
priest's mouth an incisor of prayer—he sprinkles salt on the naked child—kí
'kú lo, káá rùn lo—in a flash, the knife tears open the wrist of this child & fills
it with pruned flowers—child of lavender, sneeze!—bring from this drowning
the happiness excreted off of your mother's body—the priest washes the child's

head—what the god wants is that the poison shifts place—that the drowning body is pulled out by shadowing another alive—the ritual room in flames, the incense escapes through the window—down the river; the sun glistens on a small rock—anywhere light is found is where these gods feast—shadows flee through the walls into the hall—into the kitchen where the mother is waiting—through the small pores of her skin, the poison enters—she performs the grand gesture of falling to the ground—into the ground—into the ground.

iv

Prelude, Christmas

The mothers are weaving their hair & talking about chickens. Iya Jide, who has poultry with twelve birds, says she is ready to sell her flock. They are outside the hairdresser's shop decked in colorful *bubu*. The wall of the complex is a painting of Fela Anikulapo raising his hands in solidarity. The women talk about their husbands. Funlola says *he has brought chickens home. Two of them.* They laugh. Aunty Folake, as she is fondly called, interjects and says, *this Christmas different.* Birds are crying like birds, and the children of men speak like the children of men. No bloodstains are on the walls lined close to the river, and no child is missing. *Olúwa o sé o.* The wind outside is chilly, full of dust. Harmattan settles cold in everybody's bones. The women plait each other's hair and palm their lips with lipsticks, ready to welcome their husbands.

Ileya

With feathers in his throat, Baba Ngani Agba opens the morning. In that record, he and his apala band sing about kindreds. The music wafts sonorously from our old Kenwood speaker my father inherited from his uncle. My father, with a broom, clears cobwebs from the edges of the living room. At the end of the requiem, a loop of birdsongs. Then silence. I go outside and stretch. Smoke rises from someone's house and I tell that the goat that ate our maize has finally met fire. I walk to the back of the house and our goat is there, sitting, waiting. Teslim and his father return from Eid in their shiny orange *Up Nepa*. My irreligious father is still singing inside. Today, we pack ourselves in his golden Opel car and go to Ìjẹ̀bú. Today, I will see my grandfather's grave again and my father will tell me how he was full of flowers, how he met a strange sickness on a fateful morning as he returned from mosque, how they brought music to him at home, on his sickbed—*gángan, àlùmọ́lè àtì omele*, and a band of singers waiting for him to begin with wisdom. He will tell me how he sits among them, transcribing music as life seeps from his father's faint body one syllable at a time. Today, we will arrive at Oke-Agbo safely, and I will run to the arena to watch goats fight. They will come to look for me and find me. I will not be missing.

Waiting for Her Son

For Samson Yéròkun

When we spot the wind of sadness, it is at the door,
like something sinister twisting a knob—we go inside the house

in the muezzin's hour—a voice thins into the air from the speaker
      & calls. The sick, somewhere, is lifting itself out of bed—in his

      dream, prayer is scrubbing the sore clean—& is the answer to
the dead child whose mother is in the house. We saw

willows waiting by the window of the house—a girl serves us Cabin biscuits
      with a jug of water—I hear a droplet of tears splashing into

      the jug of water—we drink it & do not say anything. They say the dead boy
is the family's sunshine—the room is dark, & a woman, whimpering, is still in the corner

made unwhole by loss—the map on her face leads to a bush of dead things
      perhaps there were promises, perhaps there was love, perhaps

      there were plans to bless the body with bliss for Valentine
or that the boy will come into the waiting hands of his mother.

These days of varnishing

the street blossomed
in hard red soil—

       dust loathing
the wind
       rose inside it, coating

everything brown—
even the open mouth
of the woman selling fish—

       the sun
              hung inside blue clouds
      a palette of pink

      blue & white
on a soft canvas—the leafless trees surged
in air gloated with precipitation

everyone in their house

                waiting

for iftar, or the muezzin's call

some waiting for the night to come.

waiting for sleep—a pack of men has been

          looting people from their houses

so people dreamed of guns.

        i too dreamed

              of a landscape of bones.

see—our parents thought the safest

places were rooms where children

looked into their mother's eyes

        but beneath us,

             the ground is swelling—

      my father who does not believe in god

   wakes us into prayer

my mother worries

with wrinkles kneaded into her skin.

we learned every song

the shadows piped at night

the desolate streets stretching into Adamasingba

the woman pounding yam in the corridor
        could be pounding a child
        who knows what is what in these days of varnishing?—my mother says

the fathers who go out say the drainage
    swells with bones
        & sewage.

at night, we heard a scream
        that carried fear
through the language of our silence.

crickets greyed that night with stridulation
& the watchmen blew plastic whistles
        & they beat their gongs

& their steps quickened as if
they were running from their shadows—
in the morning,

my father's friend's body was lying by our door.

Year of blood

sit in the water. count your fingers. pick the fish. eat [
         ]. name the river. when you find yourself
wandering. don't go home. don't. eat from the field of
salt. ìdáró gbà 'kòkò n'ìdáró gba'dẹ. don't pluck revenge
with old bones. let the dust speak for you. turn away
from prayer when you grow tired. sit inside your grief.
light is on its way / òwúrọ̀ kùtù ni a ti ń sán imò gbígbẹ.
the bell trolls the morning. do you need light? suck the
sun stuck between your teeth. what is broken is only a
mirror. the fragment of years spent dreaming. look now,
the trees blossom in the year of blood. what fruit do you
crave? the flesh of mango or this ripeness of revenge?
do you forgive the women whose hands touched you
before you were born? who look into calabashes to
foretell the path of your star? what do we do to them
now that they are here? this is your head speaking / òjò
tó p'àlàpà ló sọ ọ d'ohun àmúgùn f'éwúrẹ. the house of
lime, the line of coat, the dime your grandmother stole
years before she turned herself away, the bad orange,
catharsis of prayer, extradition of desire / ká-fi ẹnu-á-
dákẹ, àkàrà ìyá ìsíkẹẹlì. i know hue things by name. the
words held inside incantations / ọmọ tí yóò jẹ àṣàmú,
kékeré ló ti ṣ ṣ'ẹnu ṣámúṣamú. what do you want? tell
me. this is the year of the purge, ilu tin rì ṣaaju iji lile.
the path the lightning marked. bí ṣàngó ń p'àràbà, tó
ń fà'rókò ya, bí ti igińla kọ. take the blades from the
field of salt. sing with the flock of children. bí ajá bá ń
sínwín, á m'ojú iná. the fire is quenching, where is oil?

Litany in which my father returns home safely at night

Withered & silent, the trees on the street shrink.
Everything else is hidden in the light at night—a small decibel
          of music escaping someone's window—I wonder what they are hiding
in music—what version of orgasm has the body found in an atmosphere
          of surrender. My sister's doll sits on one of the single couches. A red
ribbon longs from under the stool. Outside, a dog barks. But we don't
          know if it is truly a dog—the night so dark the lanterns scream—so
we hear mourners as they spread their mouths like wings, something broken like twig
          in their throats. My mother, gathering my brother's hair in her hand, says, *oluwa lo*
mo omo to n tun ti jigbe bayi o—abi ta lo ku? ta lo run? a tie mo mo gan bayi.
          My father saunters in, high as sky. He is home. Alive. My sister rolls from
the long brown apoche couch onto the raffia. My mother lays my brother. They all go to sleep.
          We all go to sleep.

Glossary

Adédayọ—A Yorùbá name given to sons of royal descent. It means "The crown has morphed into joy."

Adémọ́lá—A Yorùbá name whose literal meaning is "Crown tags along with wealth."

Adéwùsì—A Yorùbá name, given to sons of royal descent. The literal meaning is "Royalty multiplies."

Àgbámọ́lẹ—Also known as Ògìdo; it is a set of soft-skinned, conga-like drums original to the Yorùbá people. Unlike most drums, it is played with the hands, not sticks.

Àmàlà—A swallow meal, original to the Yorùbá ethnic group, which is made from yam flour, cassava flour, or unripe plantain flour.

Àpàlà—A socio-religious, percussion-based music genre that is specific to the Yorùbá people.

Apárí Pẹ́ńkà—The baldman of Pẹ́ńkà.

Àrólé—Heir.

As a fine boy, kò yẹ kí o ní anxiety nau—As a fine boy, you should not have anxiety.

Àti—And

Àyánwọlé—A Yorùbá name that is specific to the Àyàn lineage (which deals with affairs of drumming generally). It can be translated as "The drummer came in."

Bàbá Ńgàní Àgbà—The pseudonym for a legendary musician and Àpàlà artist, Hárúnà Ìshọ́lá Bello MON.

Bàbá ọmọ—The child's father.

Bámiṣẹ́—A Yorùbá name whose literal meaning is "Assist me in doing it." It is an abridged version of Olúwabámiṣẹ́.

Bí ajá bá ń sínwín, á m'ojú iná—A mad dog will steer clear from fire, still.

Bí Sàngó ń pàràbà, tó ń fà'rókò ya, bí ti igi iílá kọ—Even if Sàngó strikes down the kapok tree and rips the African teak tree apart, the iílá tree is always spared.

Bọ́lá Ìgè—A Nigerian lawyer, politician, and former minister of justice of Nigeria. He was assassinated in December 2001.

Bùkọ́lá—A Yorùbá name whose literal meaning is "Scoop to wealth or nobility."

Dáadáa ni—It is fine.

Dámilọ́lá—A Yorùbá name that means "(God) makes me wealthy"; an abridged version of Olúwadámilọ̀lá.

Dáramọ́lá—A Yorùbá name whose literal meaning is "One who has merged success with wealth."

Ẹ̀ bà - A swallow food made from dried, grated cassava (manioc), popularly called garri.

Ẹ gbàdúrà fún mi, Màámi—Pray for me, my mother.

Emèrè—Loosely regarded as Familiar Spirits, they are special children believed to have the ability to travel through the spiritual and physical portal at will.

Èṣù láàlú òkiri òkò—Èṣù, the honor of the city, the one whose firmness equals that of a stone.

Ẹ̀yin ènìyàn Olúwa—People of God.

Fẹlá Aníkúlápó—A legendary Nigerian musician and activist who founded Afrobeat, a Nigerian music genre.

Fẹ́lẹ̀lẹ̀—A community in Ìbàdàn, Ọ̀yọ́ state, Nigeria.

Fọlá—A Yorùbá name whose literal meaning is "To use wealth." It is usually a prefix to certain extended Yorùbá names.

Fọlákẹ—A Yorùbá name that means "Petted with wealth."

Fúnlọ́lá—A Yorùbá name that means "(To) give wealth."

Gángan - A type of talking drum, original to the Yorùbá people. It is quite portable and elevated because of its high pitch and sharp sound.

Gèlè—Head tie.

Ìbàdàn—The capital and most populous city in Ọ̀yọ́ state, located in southwestern Nigeria.

Ìdóró gba ìkòkò ni Ìdóró gba idẹ—You reap what you sow.

Ìgbà òjò ń lọ, ìgbà ẹ̀rùn ń lọ, a ní ká dí ìsà eku kó le, ìgbà wo la óò tó wá peku náà?—The rainy season passes, the autumn passes, and we ask that the rat's burrow be sealed up so that it is firm, when exactly do we get to kill the rat?

Ìjẹbú—A Yorùbá kingdom in Ògùn state, southwestern Nigeria.

Iléyá—Loosely translated as "It is time to go home," it is the Yorùbá name for the Eid el Kabir holiday observed by Muslims.

Ìlú tí ń rì ṣaájú ìjì líle—A city that sinks faster than a typhoon.

Ìrókò—The African teak tree.

Ìyá Jídé—Jídé's mother.

Ká-fi-ẹnú-á-dákẹ́, àkàrà ìyá Ìsíkíẹ̀lì—Just like the àkàrà by Ezekiel's mother, certain things are best ignored.

Kàkà ká bi ẹgbàá ọ̀bùn, ká bi ọ̀kanṣoṣo ọ̀gá, ó kúkú yá—Instead of breeding two thousand filthy ones, it is better to give birth to just one exceptional child.

Káyọ̀dé—A Yorùbá name that means "(To) arrive with joy."

Kí ikú lọ, kí ààrùn lọ—So that death may leave, so that sickness may leave.

Òde là ń ṣàgbà, ilé kan bí ibó. Bó pẹ́ títí, àtilé àtòde ni ń bọ̀ wá kan—We are bound to act as elders in public space, even if home reeks of extreme sourness. Regardless of how long it might take, home and the outside space will equally become sour.

Ọgbọn-mowò, ọmọ Èrùwà—For I've catered for thirty, o ye scions of Èrùwà.

Ògo àti àdàbà—Glory and dove.

Ògúnkọ̀yà—A Yorùbá name given to children born in households that worship the Òrìṣà Ògún, the Yorùbá deity of iron and metallurgy. The literal meaning of the name is "Ògún has rejected our sufferings."

Ògúnlẹ́yẹ—A Yorùbá name given to children born in households that worship the ancestral Òrìṣà Ògún, which is believed to oversee all affairs pertaining to metals and iron. The literal meaning of the name is "Ògún has honor."

Ogún-mobí, ọmọ koríko-- For I've given birth to twenty, o ye scions of the wild grass.

Òjò tó p'àlàpà ló sọ ọ́ d'ohun àmúgùn f'éwúrẹ—It was the rain that drenched the wall that made it a stepping stone for goats.

Òkè Àdó—A community in Ìbàdàn, Ọ̀yọ́ state, Nigeria.

Òkè Àgbò—A community in Ìjẹbú North, Ògùn state, Nigeria.

Òkè Bọ́là—A community in Ìbàdàn, Ọ̀yọ́ state, Nigeria.

Òkò lọmọ, Ọlọ́run ni ń wípé ká á sọ ọ́ síbi tó dára—A child is a flung stone, only God gets to have a final say on if it lands in a good place.

Ọládèjì—A Yorùbá name thatmeans "Wealth becomes dual."

Ọlátúnjí—A Yorùbá name that means "Wealth is awake, again."

Olúṣhọlá—A Yorùbá name that means "The prominent one makes wealth."

Olúsọjí—A Yorùbá name whose literal meaning is "The Lord has arisen."

Olúwa, níbo lójú rẹ́ wà?—Lord, where is your face situated?

Olúwa, o ṣé o—Lord, thank you.

Olúwabámiṣé—A Yorùbá name that means "God has assisted me in doing it."

Olúwa ló mọ ọmọ tọ́ tún ti jígbé báyìí o - àbí ta ló kú? Ta ló rùn? A kò tiẹ̀ mọ̀ mọ́ gan báyìí—Only the Lord knows whose child has been kidnapped now, or who died? Who stank? We do not even know anymore.

Olúwatósìn-- A Yorùbá name whose literal meaning is "God is sufficient enough to be worshipped."

Omele—The smallest drum in the Bàtá family, mostly played with two leather straps.

Ọmọ ìyá alákàrà—The àkàrà maker's offspring.

Ọmọ mi dà?—Where is my child?

Ọmọ mi—My child.

Ọmọ tí yóò jẹ àṣàmú, kékeré ni yóò ti ṣenu ṣámúṣámú—A child bound to be smart tends to exhibit this tendency at a very early stage in life.

O ní everything tí o fẹ́, ó yẹ kí o máa dúpẹ́ ni—You have everything that you want, you ought to be grateful.

Òrìṣà ilé ẹni kìí hun'ni—One's ancestral deity does not forsake one.

Orogún kìí jogún orogún—A rival does not inherit (the assets of) a fellow rival.

Oró ò!—Agony!

Òwúrọ̀ kùtù ni a ti ń sán amọ̀ gbígbẹ—We plaster the dry clay, early in the morning.

Pàrágà - An alcoholic drink.

Páríboto rìboto—A Yorùbá expression, takenfrom a folk song, that promotes the primacy of mother and child.

Şẹ́gun—A Yorùbá name that means "To conquer."

Şèyí—A Yorùbá name that serves as a suffix to other Yorùbá names situationally. The breakdown is "Do(es) this."

Şhótínbọ̀—A Yorùbá name that is specific to people who worship Òrìṣà Oko, the Yorùbá deity of agriculture and harvest. The extended morphology of the name is "Òrìṣà Oko is coming."

Síkírá—A Yorùbá corrupted version of the Arabic name Dhikrullah, which means "Remembrance" or "Recollection."

Sókà—A community in Ìbàdàn, Ọ̀yọ́ state, Nigeria.

Sùwé—Popular in the Nigerian community, Sùwé is a game played by children and teenagers that involves drawing conjoined boxes on the floor.

Tínko tínko—A two-player game, common in the Nigerian community. It involves the interchanging and clapping of hands at a quick pace.

Tínko tìnko tìnkoko tìnko—An opening lyric, rendered by people who engage in the two-player game, Tínko.

Tọ́lá—A Yorùbá name whose literal meaning is "As prominent as wealth." It is usually a prefix to certain extended Yorùbá names.

Tóyọ̀sí—A Yorùbá name that means "A child is sufficient enough to rejoice over."

Wèrè lọ́ún yà lọ yìí—She is running mad.

Yéròkun—A Yorùbá name that can be translated as "Mother went to the ocean."

Acknowledgments

It is unbelievable that this community called *The Years of Blood* is finally in your hands. Several nights of nightmares, waking up in my own sweat, hallucinating, and reliving the horrors of childhood in Ibadan, Lagos, in Iowa and New Jersey, and in the small dorms in Greensburg and Oakland. This book relies heavily on memory, and all its failures, and most of the poems were written in the heat and cold of Iowa during my MFA studies. My first thanks go to my family: Dad, Mum, Adejoke, Olapeju, Ayomide, Gbemisola, Oluwatimileyin and Danielle. I owe so many baskets of gratitude to editors and journals who accepted and published the first iterations of several poems in this collection:

World Literature Today—"Ibadan"
Consio Mag—"Soka"
Transition—"We Daydreamed of Angels" and "Migration"
Minnesota Review—"Unfound"
Poetry Magazine—"Prelude, Christmas," "The Abduction," and "Before the Dark"
Ex Puritan—"The Dark"
Anmly—"Fine Boy Writes a Poem about Anxiety"
Tab: The Journal of Poetry & Poetics— "Wishbone"
Southern Indiana Review—"Doomsday"
Isele Magazine—"Portent" and "Arrival"
Statement of Record—"Two Boys, Their Mother & the Face"
Wildness—"Litany in Which My Father Returns Home Safely at Night"
Frontier Poetry—"Lilac"

My unreserved thanks go to Elisabeth Frost and JoAnne McFarland for seeing this book, selecting it, and acknowledging the heaviness it carries and how it seeks to heal the world by documenting. I am also thankful to Alex Tischer for all that he does.

To Richard Morrison, publisher of Fordham University Press, and Sarah Gambito, Director of Creative Writing at Fordham University, thank you for your patience and the care with which you handled the book. I also express my gratitude to the editorial board at Fordham, including Tamiko Beyer, Janlori Goldman, Cynthia Hogue, Deborah Paredez, and Roger Reeves.

I wrote "Ìbàdàn" on the flight to Chicago, on my way to Iowa to begin the MFA program at the Iowa Writers Workshop. I am most thankful to Tracie Morris, in whose workshop this book began to form. I remember the heaviness in the room when we read "Arrival." Thank you for your motherly love and blessing. I thank Mark Levine, who, one evening before graduation, said, "My friend, stay in touch. We were lucky you came here." Mark, I am fortunate to have worked with you. Your line edits changed my perspectives on sentences and the worlds we build inside them. Special thanks to Elizabeth Willis, my professor and thesis chair, whose care, attention, and edits formed conversations that firmly built this book. Elizabeth, I am grateful for your poems, leadership, and mentorship. I will forever be your student.

I thank my peers at the Iowa Writers Workshop. We cried together, thought together, discussed, and arrived through our rootedness and love for poetry. Kyra Spence, Margaret Yapp, Nicole Adabunu, Tramaine Suubi, Tess Caroll, Elise Bickford, Trevor Kildiszew, Olivia Tse, Kami Nzeribe, Alessandra Leigh Allen, and many more—for your poems, friendship, and all the drinks you bought me.

To Adams Adeosun, the gatherer of my falling apart, may the universe answer you. Othuke Umukoro, Okwudili Nebolisa, Adeniyi Ademoroti, Mofiyinfoluwa Okupe, Reyumeh Ejue, Otosirieze Obi-Young, and Romeo Oriogun, the memories of Iowa's cold is warm because you all were there.

I am so grateful to Remica Bingham-Risher, whose wisdom, edits, arrangement, love, and support ushered this book into the world. And to all my Cave Canem Family, thank you for providing space to be African and myself, write in Greenburg's whistling morning, and sit outside with you and study the weather. Special thanks to my past faculty and board members: Major Jackson, Durriel Harris, Tracie Morris, Janice Harrington, Matthew Shenoda, Kwame Dawes, Lynne Thompson, Tyehimba Jess, and A. Van Jordan. Toi Derricotte and Cornelius Eady, you have built a city that will never go to ruins. Salawu Olajide, thank you for your brotherhood, comradeship, and blessings. Your impact on *The Years of Blood* cannot be measured. Funsho Oris, Jide Badmus, Jumoke Verissimo, Dami Ajayi, Gbenga Adesina, DM Aderibigbe, Samson Kukogbo, Kola Tunbosun, Iquo DianaAbasi Eke, and Ukamaka Olisakwe, I am grateful to be connected to you all in some way. Your generosity and mentorship has shaped the poet that I am today.

I send all praise and accolades to my literary agent, Salma Begum, of the Greyhound Literary Agency, for saying yes even before the sun started to rise—for seeing everything green when the field was bland.

Unreserved thanks to the leadership and faculty of the Wallace Stegner Fellowship at Stanford University: Nicholas Jenkins, A. Van Jordan, Molly Antopol, Aracelis Girmay, Adam Johnson, Chang-Rae Lee, Patrick Phillips, and Elizabeth Tallent. Love and respect to Wallace Stegner Fellows, your friendship and wisdom always, through thick and slice: Luciana Arbus-Scandiffio, Stephanie Horvath, Fatima Jafar, Weijia Pan, Joseph Rios, D. M. Spratley, Bernardo Wade, Dāshaun Washington, Hua Xi. Jade Cho, Madeleine Cravens, Jalen Eutsey, Christell Victoria Roach, and D. S. Waldman. The Bay Area is not the same without you. I am sincerely thankful for how your comments, advice, and brilliance have contributed to this book. I also cannot forget the kindnesses of Christina Ablaza, Danielle Huliganga, and Mailan Smith.

Finally, to my friends: Dr. Njera Fraiser, Joel Komlan, Ariana Benson, Yusuf Gemini, Tawanda Hauwa Shaffi Nuhu, Mulalu, Frances Ogamba, Mubanga Kalimamukwento, Kányinsọlá Ọlọrunnísọlá, Oyindamola Shoola, Olowere Kosemani, Monisola Olomola, Sherry Mo, Ashley Zhang, Kayode Kareem, Ademola Adepoju, Ayomide Festus, Ayomide Agarau, Damilola Mobee, and Ufoma Gloria, among others. To the soldiers of Nigerian poetry, members of the UnSerious Collective, Nome Emeka Patrick, O-Jeremiah Agbaakin, Wale Ayinla, Michael Akuchie, Pamilerin Jacob, and Kolawole Adebayo, may you never toil in vain.

Adedayo Agarau is a Wallace Stegner Fellow '25, a Cave Canem Fellow, and a 2024 Ruth Lilly-Rosenberg Fellowship finalist. He is the Editor-in-Chief of *Agbowó Magazine: A Journal of African Literature and Art* and a Poetry Reviews Editor for *The Rumpus*. He is the author of the chapbooks *Origin of Name* (African Poetry Book Fund, 2020) and *The Arrival of Rain* (Vegetarian Alcoholic Press, 2020). For more information, visit www.adedayoagarau.com.

POETIC JUSTICE INSTITUTE

Adedayo Agarau
The Years of Blood

Marcella Durand
A Winter Triangle
foreword by Srikanth Reddy